BREATHE

A VISION & FRAMEWORK FOR HUMAN-CENTERED LEARNING ENVIRONMENTS

DR. BERNARD BULL

Birdhouse Learning Labs, LLC
11561 North Buntrock Avenue
Mequon, WI 53092

www.birdhouselearninglabs.com
Printed in the United States of America
Cover by Riki Unrau.
ISBN 978-1-7333201-4-6 (ebook) First Edition
ISBN 978-1-7333201-5-3 (print) First Edition

INTRODUCTION

In the early 2000s, I embarked on a quest. I launched a research project to explore and understand the breadth and depth of possibilities for the future of education. This exploration eventually led me to visit and study over a hundred schools and conduct more than a thousand formal and informal interviews with people involved with education reform, innovation, entrepreneurship, and re-imagining both learning experiences and learning communities. In turn, I was drawn to schools and learning communities that were often void of things like desks in rows, bells, letter grades, and discipline-specific courses. I explored different facets of learning: online, blended, project-based, problem-based, place-based, arts-immersion, self-directed, and I examined many models, frameworks, and practices.

One of the first schools that I visited was George D. Warriner High School, a personalized and project-based-learning school in Sheboygan, Wisconsin. I first learned about the school when I came across a doctoral dissertation by a student at Pepperdine University. The author, George D. Warriner, offered a vision for a new model of school, one that tapped into the personal passions and interests of each learner. I soon discovered that this dissertation inspired the launch of a school. While the visionary of the school passed away far too young, he shared the dream with others who went on to lead and further bring this school into reality.

At the time, I lived an hour away from George D. Warriner High, and after reading the dissertation, I wanted to see it for myself. A brief phone conversation with the principal led to an invitation to visit and experience it myself. I readily accepted, and the next week, I drove up and got a glimpse, ever-so-small, of what they were doing. Each student proposed a project or plan for the semester's learning after completing a required twenty-first-century skills course that equipped them for this radical self-direction and personalization. However, there were no traditional, content-area courses or curriculum. The school was void of conventional classrooms and teachers. Learners explored everything from music to anthropology, popular culture to religion. There were no instructor-led groups of students to be found; rather, they collaborated in small groups or worked individually. Active and engaged, they took ownership of their learning.

Prior to this visit, I hadn't experienced a project-based-learning environment, but driving home that day, memories of that visit inspired me. George D. Warriner High School was just one of hundreds or thousands of other rich, vibrant learning communities where voice, choice, ownership, and agency were central. That couldn't be an isolated community, but it *was* what I wanted for my daughter—to see learning and knowledge as rich, rewarding, engaging, and empowering. Every child should have the opportunity to learn in ways that tap into his or her deepest needs and yearnings as a human being and that treats each child as a unique individual, loved, full of potential, and inspired to discover particular callings and roles in the world.

That was one stop of many. That first visit and collection of interviews soon turned into studying a myriad of schools throughout the United States and other parts of the world. Every week, I tried to discover, reach out to, interview, and whenever possible, visit other learning communities. George D. Warriner High School was not a unique case. These incredibly engaging and beautifully humane schools existed all around, and there was no reason why they couldn't become the norm.

Writing about my findings led to speaking invitations at conferences throughout the United States and beyond. My mission was simple and direct—invite people to consider the breadth of possibilities, convinced that if people knew what was possible, it would lead them to incorporate some of that innovation into their classrooms and schools. For some—sometimes a solitary teacher, other times an entire school or new school launch—it did, and I was honored to have played even a small part in helping people envision new ways of teaching and learning.

Only, as I discovered and shared more, I did so even as another trend gained increasing dominance. Debates grew about and drove attention toward themes: Common Core State Standards, standardized testing, and the regulatory pressures on schools from the state and federal level. Over a decade, teacher education in the United States became increasingly focused upon practices shaped by standardization, quantification, and other industrial priorities. Teachers lamented their lack of freedom and creativity. And even for those not directly impacted by these growing trends, I witnessed schools and educators—from elementary through the graduate level—unnecessarily limited to a narrow set of possibilities that fit inside the traditions and standard policies and practices.

That was the point I realized that merely helping people explore the options was no longer enough. Current traditions, policies, and practices were holding people back. If I genuinely wanted to contribute to a qualitatively better, more hopeful, humane, engaging, and inspiring academic ecosystem, I needed to find a way to offer educators a framework to get there.

That was just the beginning.

This short text is a simple set of priorities that I contend can replace the dominant educational priorities of today. For each theme, I also offer questions that the reader can ask to embrace these ideals in a single classroom, a school, a district, or an entire education ecosystem. My goal in this book is to introduce a new framework, but over the upcoming years, to also create guides, templates, exemplars, resources, and other tools that help schools and educators move from the aspirational to the actual. My goal is no less than to offer an alternative to the persistent and industrial priorities and to begin to provide steps toward embodying that alternative.

PART I

WHAT IS IN THE AIR?

WHAT IS IN THE AIR?

It starts with subtle physiological changes that mostly go unnoticed, beginning with impaired thinking and attention. People find it difficult to complete otherwise easy tasks. From there, we notice an ongoing downward decline that includes poor judgment, exhaustion, and difficulty in managing emotions; even the simplest of comments can spark an outburst of anger. Eventually, they find it hard to stay awake. Unfortunately, this sequence of events is far too common. We see it in schools, classrooms, workplaces, and sometimes even in the more private portions of our existence. Yet, that description comes from a clinical definition of hypoxia, oxygen deficiency.

Too many learners and teachers are going through significant parts of their lives, struggling with symptoms associated with a lack of fundamental human needs: the social, emotional, intellectual, even spiritual equivalents of oxygen. What is even more fascinating is that we have created systems where we blame victims for their symptoms. We don't blame people for experiencing the symptoms of hypoxia, but society is often quick to cast judgment when the equivalent occurs in schools, workplaces, and other parts of our lives. It isn't oxygen that we crave, but there is an obvious deficiency in the educational air.

Learners in the modern school system, who experience similar symptoms are likely living in the intellectual and emotional equivalent of an oxygen-deprived community or context. The solution is not to adapt to less air. It is to pump air into the classroom. Even if every system can't be changed, there is a way to provide personal air tanks so that learners can thrive regardless of the context. That mask can be worn to breathe deeply and flourish while others struggle to stay motivated, can't remember what was just said, or fail to experience the beauty and fullness of the moment. It is time to breathe.

The word "inspire" means to "breathe in" or to "inhale." This book is about helping to understand and identify why so many schools and classrooms are uninspired, leaving people gasping for air.

Breathe: A Vision and Framework for Human-Centered Learning Environments examines seven reasons for oxygen-deprived schools and explores seven ways to add inspiration to our learning communities—practices and priorities that are central to the human experience, providing the emotional and intellectual equivalent of air. When we breathe these qualities into our classrooms, something amazing begins to happen.

Interestingly, the factors that suck the oxygen from our schools are good, often contributing to health, healing, safety, order, and so much more. As you'll learn in subsequent pages, I'm referring to ideas like efficiency, order, and measurement. Rather than being bad, we are discussing concepts that play a part in imagining new possibilities and creating solutions to some of our most significant problems in society. The difficulty is that many of these ideals that provide immense value when trying to solve a mechanical or systemic problem are incapable of breathing life into our schools. And yet, these industrial ideals are too often emphasized when it comes to time, attention, concern, and money in education. **We have mistaken the supporting elements as foundational and treated the truly foundational elements as if they were secondary niceties.** Neither is true, and our education ecosystem will continue to struggle if we allow this pattern of thought to dominate.

In a moment, I will outline the seven industrial priorities in contemporary education and build, what I hope to be, a compelling case for a different way forward. When used as supporting priorities, industrial values like efficiency and measurement are valuable and powerful. When we make them central, we unintentionally create the equivalent of an oxygen-deficient-learning experience and community.

These seven oxygen-depriving factors grew out of rapid scientific and industrial developments in the seventeenth and eighteenth centuries. While not an exhaustive list, this text examines seven: the pursuit of standardization and uniformity, mass production and scalability, efficiency and order, centralized power and control, mechanization and automation, and quantification. Looking at this list, our world is shaped and continually reshaped by the influence of these priorities. They are critically important. The problem is that these industrial ideas are incapable of leading to an inspired learning community. They transform societies and the people in those societies, but when they dominate, they leave us gasping for our next breath.

PART II

WHAT IS A PRIORITY & WHY DOES IT MATTER?

WHAT IS A PRIORITY & WHY DOES IT MATTER?

By definition, a priority is that which we regard as more or most important. When something is a priority, it shapes the questions that people ask, muzzling other questions. Look at the recent conversations in the modern education system. There are countless and competing beliefs about what type of education is best, but regardless of the position someone holds, notice how almost all of the public debate centers around test scores on the elementary and secondary school levels and on graduation rates, job placement, and post-graduation salary for colleges. There are plenty of other viewpoints. Still, the easily testable and quantifiable parts are such a high priority that people across positions find themselves using the same benchmarks. These are useful tools, but they are not the only measures. In fact, some of the most critical elements of an inspired learning community are difficult to quantify, which may be part of why they get muzzled.

Consider an example outside of education. For decades, the dominant measure for the health of a country was the gross domestic product (GDP), the total monetary value of goods and services provided by a country in a given year.

Since this measure was the priority, it focused conversations and efforts on trying to increase the GDP of a nation, drawing attention away from other factors and reducing health to a matter of money. Eventually, a growing number of scholars asserted that the health of a nation calls for looking at much more than just the economy. There is a need to take into account factors like life expectancy, freedom, positive relationships, and evidence of generosity. Notice how adding these other considerations completely shifts the conversation, leading to thoughts about the health of a nation in terms of happiness and well-being and not simply in terms of economics. This is precisely how priorities work in education, and it is why this is such an important topic.

It does not matter how well-intended the education reform; if we don't reconsider the underlying priorities, any attempted change will ultimately fail. Imagine an innovative school that replaces most traditional lectures with rich and engaging projects and student-centered learning. Yet, at the end of the course, students are given the same multiple-choice exam that existed before the change. If students perform poorly on the test, many are likely to judge this innovation as a failure. The problem is that the traditional test might not be a good measure of what students learned with the new project-based approach. There was a change in practice, but not a change in priority.

Even some of the most intriguing and alternative elementary and secondary schools today turn to test scores when they want to make a public case about the efficacy of their approach. The problem is that these tests fail to measure what is most valued in many of these new approaches. Interestingly, a school created as an intentional contrast to the larger, test-driven system still finds itself drawn into the test-dominant mindset. There are plenty of examples of leading critics of standardized testing who oddly use standardized test scores to defend their educational point of view. Perhaps that is just an exercise in speaking the language of the other side of the issue, but it also reveals what is primary and what is secondary in the system.

This is not limited to schools. We see the focus upon quantification in the workplace and even our lives. As with the other six industrial priorities, it is not bad. It is a gift that helps us achieve any number of worthwhile goals. It is just that the drive to quantify everything makes a terrible leader. Alone, it lacks humanity. It lacks life.

When these industrial concepts take control of our education system, they become the shapers of the climate and culture, turning into the rulers by which society measures quality and success—good or bad. What follows is a demand for the majority of time, attention, and money.

Alone, industrial values are incapable of connecting the most basic human yearnings. In contrast, and regardless of an individual's belief system, certain human desires persist across time and culture. Glimpses of them can be seen in art and literature from around the world—from 2000 BCE to yesterday—they are present and breathe life into people, places, societies, and civilizations. Because they are so fundamental to the human experience, when they are present in adequate amounts, they engage and inspire.

Today, we find evidence for these cravings in both ancient wisdom and the most cutting-edge research on the psychology of well-being. They are all over the pages of the most beloved stories and myths across cultures and time, even in the sacred texts of ancient religious traditions. Simultaneously, researchers in growing areas of study like positive psychology are discovering increasingly compelling evidence of how they are powerful forces for human flourishing.

While there are many, I've selected seven for this book, each of which consistently contributes to the equivalent of educational oxygen. They include **adventure and quests, agency and action, compassion and connectedness, experimentation and play, mastery and growth, meaning and purpose, wonder and mystery.** These pump oxygen into our schools. When learners breathe deeply, they quickly find themselves more alert, more motivated, more alive.

The goal of this book is simply to offer a tour of the seven industrial priorities that unintentionally lead to less-inspired living. This includes celebrating the good that they create in the world but also recognizing the risks and shortfalls. Then, in the last part of the book, there is a vision for what is possible when educators and school leadership focus on seven human-centered priorities. This is an invitation to breathe deeply, to embrace and enjoy a growing measure of inspiration.

I wrote this book with the conviction that less is more. A thousand-page book on human schooling will not solve the problem. What we need is a greater awareness of what leads to perpetual disappointment with schools combined with some practical steps for what to do about it. The most exciting part comes each time readers set this book down and breathe.

In fact, consider a simple exercise. Close your eyes. Stand up. Inhale deeply and then slowly exhale. Do it a couple of times. That oxygen you inhale fuels your entire body with what it craves and needs for life. That is precisely the goal of this book. Throughout the pages, focus your attention on how to create schools and classrooms where everyone breathes more deeply, where they find themselves enjoying the benefits that come from simply inhaling that which humans desire, that which leads to inspired learning.

PART III

OXYGEN DEFICIENCY

STANDARDIZATION AND UNIFORMITY

"Sour, sweet, bitter, pungent, all must be tasted."

— CHINESE PROVERB

This is a standardized world, so much so that people hardly recognize it. Industries agree upon specifics for the size, shape, and other features that make it easy to find a battery replacement, screw, or a missing piece from a favorite gadget.

Uniformity allows people to speak a common language and to add consistency across time and place. If you need to charge your cell phone, if you have the proper cord and charger, you can do it almost anywhere, thanks to standards. The same is true if you need healthcare and are traveling from one place to another—standard practices.

The ability to read the words in this text comes from a shared understanding of certain rules that govern grammar, spelling, and syntax. You can pick up almost any work written

DR. BERNARD BULL

in English and make sense of it because of language standards. From the sixteenth century to the present, we see thousands of movements toward uniform English spelling, and the same thing happened in many other languages as well.

Standardization and uniformity create enormous benefits for society. They help improve quality, increase the ability to connect and communicate across organizations and people, enhance productivity, give people a sense of safety, and even improve morale in the workplace. When there are practices and policies in place, people know what to expect, thereby reducing confusion and anxiety.

There is a dark side to all of this structure. Without negating the benefits, consider these questions. Who decides upon the standards in the first place? Which voices are heard and celebrated? Which views are rarely invited or considered? What happens when there is a brilliant but non-uniform practice or action? Standardization always includes some measure of politics and power, and that means winners and losers.

When a compulsion for sameness takes over a community, context, or classroom, some things get amplified and others muzzled. Again, there is good that comes from standardization. Still, there is also an incredible amount of beauty and rich meaning that comes from celebrating and attending to that which is not consistent. Variety is the opposite of uniformity. Antonyms for "standard" include words like exceptional, extraordinary, strange, unconventional, unorthodox, and rare. Imagining life without those seems odd. So, when standardization and makers become the highest priority in a school, we start to lose some of the very things that excite, interest, intrigue, and inspire—the synonyms of life.

The goal isn't to get rid of standards and uniformity, it is to put them into perspective, to create space in schools for variety, the extraordinary, and unconventional. We want to value these enough that we find ourselves appreciating and celebrating them rather than simply judging almost every-thing around us based on whether it is standard. We can appreciate the role of standards and uniformity in some aspects while making sure we create plenty of space for the exceptional, extraordinary, strange, unconventional, unortho-dox, and rare.

MASS PRODUCTION AND SCALABILITY

B igger is better. If you can produce one item, what will it take to create a thousand or a million? That is the mass-production mindset. It is a focus on how to take what you are doing and turn it into a global enterprise.

As soon as you start thinking about how to mass produce something, you also need to think about how to eliminate the anomalies and outliers. So, the priority of mass production is closely tied to standardization and uniformity, just as it is with the next priority, efficiency and order.

What does mass production have to do with our schools? It is the spirit and mindset that shapes so much of modern education and workplace environments and influences so much of our lives.

As sociologist George Ritzer wrote, it represents the *McDonaldization of Society*. MacDonald's is a classic example of mass production, a restaurant experience that Ritzer describes as reduced to an effort for the most efficient way to get people from hungry to full. "Fast food" is all about creating a refined production process that gets food to the consumer quickly, at a low price, and a level of quality that satisfies the customer's hunger. On any given day, a mass-production restaurant serves far more people than almost all the traditional ones. People have come to accept and value these expressions of mass production.

Humans crave meaning and are incredibly resilient, so even when restaurants are reduced or redesigned in such a way, we see people strive to create meaning and purpose in them. Again, this is not to say that fast food is inherently bad. It is merely an expression of a mass-production value that holds a place of priority and privilege in today's society.

You are probably a part of one or more mass-production machines, or at least you have been one at some point in your life. For most, that started with school, a system that teaches individuals to accept and function as part of a mass-produced system. We teach children to stand and patiently wait in a single file line, a mass-production fundamental that continues far beyond school years. Kids are seated in single file rows in classrooms. Think about how student bodies learn to move from place to place at the ringing of a bell or seamlessly through the cafeteria line. In fact, by the time teenagers graduate from high school, they've likely had that response reinforced over 16,000 times. Even when it comes to communicating and documenting performance in school, students receive a letter or number ranking, a similar system to how we rate milk, meat, and eggs in the world of mass production.

Mass production and scale historically depend upon homogeneity, sameness. That becomes valued and celebrated over diversity and variety, which takes us back to the last priority of standardization and uniformity. It reminds us of the central theme in Malvina Reynold's song, performed by Pete Seeger in 1963, "And the people in the houses all went to the University where they were put in boxes and they came out all the same..."

As with all these industrial priorities, they create benefits for people and societies, and for most places in the world, they are not going away soon. What is essential to recognize is that by themselves, they are incapable of breathing oxygen into our schools. The challenge is to figure out how to give equal voice to the value and beauty of one-of-a-kind, handcrafted, boutique education and thinking, and we see that happening.

Even as mass production continues to expand, we see parallel movements like makerspaces, farm-to-table restaurants, and a growing appreciation of handcrafted works. In education, there is the growth of micro-schools with distinct niches, the rapid rise of homeschooling, and self-directed and learner-driven communities, where students are co-creators of what and how they learn, and where we celebrate distinct gifts and interests.

This is a natural expression of the human yearning for more of what breathes life into the learning experience. Even in the most mass-produced contexts, people strive to find ways to create meaning and purpose, to tap into that which inspires them. Some who see mass production as the priority sometimes define these human expressions as a rebellion against the system. What if they are simply the relentless urge to infuse more life into their learning, like a flower growing up through the crack of a cement walkway.

That is a helpful metaphor for thinking about how those in pursuit of inspired learning communities might want to think about living in an increasingly mass-produced education system. Look for the cracks in the cement. Look for the pockets where humanity can grow, even if everything else around it is a cold, hard sidewalk.

EFFICIENCY AND ORDER

"The worst enemy of life, freedom, and the common decencies is total anarchy; their second worst enemy is total efficiency."

— ALDOUS HUXLEY

The mission of an efficiency-focused person or organization is to accomplish tasks with the least amount of wasted time, money, effort, or energy. Jacques Ellul wrote that "Modern technology has become a total phenomenon for civilization, the defining force of a new social order in which efficiency is no longer an option but a necessity imposed on all human activity."

Most of us see the benefits of efficiency. If we want to get to work in the morning, unless we have time and interest in a scenic trip, we seek out the fastest route from home to work. Parents plan meals in advance, divide up responsibilities and chores to accomplish in the household, and look for ways to simplify tasks. That is part of managing the competing priorities in a busy life.

Only some of the most memorable moments come from embracing a measure of inefficiency in our lives as well. Sometimes completing a task in a way that takes more time, costs more money, and requires more energy can, in the long run, produce a greater result. A narrow view of efficiency can prevent people from ever experiencing such moments.

Order is beautiful. There is something incredibly satisfying about cleaning a room or office or adding order to a seemingly cluttered and disorganized collection of items. That is why some people like solving puzzles and problems. We are creating and discovering meaning, and as we will explore later in this book, meaning is pure oxygen to the human spirit.

Random is beautiful, too. Consider the unpredictability and ambiguity of parenting, long-lasting friendships, and embracing the challenge to solve a puzzle or create something that does not yet exist. Or focusing more upon learning, consider the long, messy, delightful, agonizing journey from novice to expert in almost any field or discipline. Getting to the order calls for a tolerance of the disorder for a period of time, maybe even an appreciation of it, and a recognition that it will never go away. In fact, trying to sort and organize something too quickly might hinder the process of developing a deep and nuanced understanding of a subject. It is one thing to study a forest. It is a completely different thing to cut down all the trees and sort them by size and type.

Robert Kenney once stated that "Democracy is messy, and it's hard. It's never easy." This relates to one of the most important recent books written about the history of American higher education, David Labaree's, *A Perfect Mess: The Unlikely Ascendancy of American Higher Education*. A central message in the literature is that American higher education is a history of occasional chaos, failed experiments, diversity, inconsistencies, and largely a "system without a plan." In an interview, I once asked David what he would do to destroy or undermine the American college and university system. He said that he would remove the messiness and demand a clean and standard system, explaining that the variety and decentralized nature of American higher education is what has allowed it to grow into such a rich and diverse ecosystem.

This idea is not only for schools. Leaving room for inefficiencies in our lives is also what creates fertile soil for rich and inspired living. This is not a call for the abandonment of order. It is an invitation to resist a monopoly, to leave space for the beautiful and serendipitous moments that come from embracing complexity.

QUANTIFICATION AND MEASUREMENT

Some say that people measure what they value. If that is the case, then what do you measure about the people who mean the most to you in life? How do you count the depth of your love for and commitment to family? How much time and energy do you devote to calculating meaning and purpose in your life? Measurement and quantification are all around us, and, as with all the industrial priorities, they play a useful and important role. They do not, however, provide what the mind, heart, and spirit crave at the most fundamental level. And measurement is not necessarily an indication of what is most important in our lives.

From our earliest days in school, students learn, even if not directly, that knowledge, performance, and intelligence can be carefully ranked and rated. There are A, B, C, D, and F students. A 95% on a test means success, and a 50% means failure. A high class rank earns preference in the top colleges. Later, students learn to determine net worth with a basic calculation. Just subtract a person's liabilities from assets. We also measure health by a series of numbers on test results. Compare those to a given scale as a means of health or sickness. These are a few aspects of life in an increasingly quantified world, and there is a compelling case that some of these measurements create far more benefits than downsides.

Measurements themselves, however, do little to inspire or breathe life. The inspiration doesn't come unless, or until, we translate the numbers into stories and meaning is created, when people use them to accomplish a noble task, when they are part of a quest to solve a complex problem. It is then that people find themselves motivated and engaged.

If we reduce the goal to getting a good grade or reaching a particular score, we've extracted the authenticity from the learning community. This is when we start to see the "good students" focusing all of their thinking and energy on the tasks and behaviors required to earn an *A* instead of what it takes to solve a problem, master a skill, or even just experience the profound joy of encountering truth, beauty, and happiness. The very fact that some educators will read that last sentence and describe it as detached from the reality of the real-world classroom is further evidence of how much we have prioritized quantification.

It's easy to become preoccupied with rating and ranking to the point of losing track of the story, the actual meaning, or the problem that we are trying to solve. It is commonplace, over time, to conflate the numbers with the story, meaning, or purpose. The learner becomes driven to earn a certain score more than to deepen understanding, or to master new knowledge and skill. The worker is more fixated on earning a higher salary than achieving larger life goals. The person originally in pursuit of health and wellness is more obsessed with counting calories and weight on a scale than achieving a more complete picture of physical well-being. It need not be an either/or, but especially when it comes to education, we want to make sure that we don't lose the meaning in the measuring.

We've all experienced this. There is something in us that is often fueled by the drive for growth, and documenting our progress can be a means of helping us determine if we are improving because growth is an oxygen-infusing element of education. The problem is that reducing everything to grades, points, and percentages fails to tell the entire story, and if we are not careful, we can find ourselves craving and running after the grades and forgetting about what ultimately matters.

CENTRALIZED POWER AND CONTROL

"I know of no safe depository of the ultimate powers of the society but the people themselves; and if we think them not enlightened enough to exercise their control with a wholesome discretion, the remedy is not to take it from them but to inform their discretion."

— THOMAS JEFFERSON

Do what I say, when I say, and how I say it. There are certainly situations where such a centralized authority works well. It might even save lives. Perhaps in an emergency, a single person has the knowledge and skill needed to get everyone through it. Or maybe it is a situation where there are complex factors, what happens in one area impacts what happens in another. People in the individual areas don't see the big picture or how things are interrelated, so they decide that it is best to go with a centralized approach.

There is even something comforting about being a good

follower, doing what the person or persons in charge command. If the leaders have your best interest in mind, and you trust these leaders, being a good follower can be comforting. I'm not about to argue against the blessings and benefits of having good, great, and wise leaders.

"Laws control the lesser man... Right conduct controls the greater one."

— MARK TWAIN

It is tempting to make centralized power and control among the highest priorities in schools. There is a propensity to glamorize the image of quiet, obedient students who carefully await the instructions of the teacher. Some educators, keen to "tightly hold the reigns" in the classroom, find themselves defining their quality as a teacher by how well they control the class.

As with each of these industrial priorities, there are benefits and limitations. Ensuring a safe and positive learning environment is arguably an important goal, but we fall short when we conflate centralized power and control with the achievement of that goal. There are alternatives.

For those who have not witnessed a quality, project-based learning environment, it might be difficult to imagine, but once a person sees it, it is hard not to be inspired. Students share power and control. They take ownership of their learning, helping and collaborating with one another, monitoring their use of time, and passionately pursuing something of importance to them. They are not only learning about whatever subject is central to the project. They are also learning about self-regulation, shared power and decision-making, and countless other ways of thinking and being that are critical to any nation with democratic values. This is what we must infuse into our schools, even as there is the sometimes-competing interest in centralized power and control.

MECHANIZATION AND AUTOMATION

"Mechanization best serves mediocrity."

— FRANK LLOYD WRIGHT

Mechanization is the shift from completing tasks by hand to doing something with machinery. Through mechanization, we can do more for less money and in less time. Depending upon the machine and task, some machines do the work of twenty, two-hundred, or two-thousand people today. Since the beginning of the industrial revolution, mechanization has been both praised for its improvements in efficiency and productivity and lamented for displacing workers, disrupting the complex and more human-centered interactions in society, and often contributing to pollution or other environmental problems.

Most of us find ourselves so immersed in an automated world that we cannot or do not imagine any other way of living. Washing machines and dishwashers replaced hand-washing for many. Modern heating units keep many warm without anyone needing to chop wood or do anything directly to replenish the heater other than writing a check to the utility company.

Mechanization and automation are on the rise in education as well, and they will not go away soon. In fact, I contend that the goal in learning communities should not be to fight against mechanization and automation as much as to take the time to consider the benefits and limitations, as well as to think about how we can maintain the oxygen-infusing priorities of life in an increasingly mechanized and automated world.

"War is the supreme drama of a completely mechanized society."

— LEWIS MUMFORD

TECHNOLOGY

"Men have become the tools of their tools."

— HENRY DAVID THOREAU

Technology is a gift, and in its simplest form, we can define it as applied scientific or systematic knowledge. It includes everything from the computers and devices we use daily to the complex systems used to design buildings, bridges, roads, hospitals, schools, businesses, and the ever-growing number of digital environments and platforms.

It would be too simplistic to talk about technology as good or bad. Some might lament how they think the increasingly digital nature of life is changing or harming relationships and personal connections or decreasing our human connections, while others are quick to point out how new media and innovations serve as a means of building and extending existing and new connections. When talking about technology in our lives, it is rarely, if ever, a simple matter.

What is true of any technology is that it has what some refer to as affordances and limitations. It makes some things more possible while making other things less possible. It amplifies some ideas while muzzling others. It creates a mix of benefits and downsides. The cell phone gives us a constant connection with people around the world, access to knowledge and people whenever and wherever we need it. It also makes it easier for us to attend to the person a thousand miles away as much or more than the person two feet from us. Simply having that option changes us, and it is hard to tell when or how that occurs.

The technologies that we use, over time, begin to influence how we think, our choices, and sometimes our decisions. A brain that grows up on video games and social media is physically different than one that grew up on wandering through the woods and playing pretend with friends in the backyard. Instead of focusing energy on whether one is better than the other, consider a posture of simple curiosity, a desire to understand what is different, to persistently explore the benefits and limitations.

In 2019, I chose to move a thousand miles away from home to accept a new job, while my family stayed behind, at least for the first nine months. I made this decision aware of how easy it was to fly back and forth and to interact with my family through video conferencing, texting, and the phone. I probably would not have taken the job without those opportunities. Still, the reality is that living 1000 miles away from my family—even with the technological means of staying connected—changed our family and me. Was it better or worse? Was it the right decision?

Technology can't answer those questions. As much as modern innovations and devices hold values within them, and as much as they shape and influence us, the technologies themselves are not the air that we crave. They only inspire when combined with something more, a noble quest, a grand mystery, the deeply human yearning for play and experimentation, meaningful connections with other people, the drive to solve a wicked problem, or a more profound sense of meaning or purpose. These spark our imaginations and inspire us to invent and create, but the technologies themselves are not what inspires. At best, they are a container or amplifier for what resides deeper within in, those deeply human yearnings that breathe life into our world.

"Science and technology revolutionize our lives, but memory, tradition, and myth frame our response."

— ARTHUR M. SCHLESINGER

PART IV

OXYGEN-RICH LEARNING COMMUNITIES

OXYGEN-RICH LEARNING COMMUNITIES

Now that we've spent time considering some of the dominant industrial priorities of our modern education system, let's turn our attention to the alternatives, the types of priorities where there is compelling evidence that they offer the promise to infuse the intellectual, emotional, even spiritual equivalent of oxygen into our learning, classrooms, and schools.

This is far from an exhaustive list. Instead, I offer these as a starting point. There are many other oxygen-infusing priorities worthy of our consideration, but I selected these seven because I believe they provide a common ground. They are each priorities that I believe will more readily resonate with the vast majority of readers and educators.

ADVENTURE AND QUESTS

"The big question is whether you are going to be able to say a hearty yes to your adventure."

— JOSEPH CAMPBELL

L ife is a collection of quests and adventures, if only we see it as such. For some, it might entail a call to a far-away place, but it might also be a journey in your backyard, an inner adventure that you can embrace and pursue from the living room. This begs the question, what is a quest or adventure?

In his book, *The Happiness of Pursuit*, Chris Guillebeau describes a quest as "the pursuit of a long-term challenge or adventure with a series of intermediate steps." Quests tend to have three elements. There is a clear mission or goal. It is a challenging goal. Then there are milestones along the way.

If we draw from the lessons of Joseph Campbell as he describes *The Hero's Journey*, there are other elements as well.

It all begins with a person living in the ordinary world until, one day, there is a call to adventure. With the call comes a struggle. Will I heed the call or not? Do I have what it takes? Is the mission or reward worth the risks? Amid this struggle, the hero-in-the-making meets a mentor or guide who offers insight, builds confidence or competence, and maybe even offers one or more gifts for the journey. Eventually, the hero faces an event or moment that leads to embracing the mission, venturing beyond the ordinary world.

Moving beyond the ordinary world and into this special world, the hero encounters tests and trials, meets and connects with allies, and faces enemies. While all of this is part of the quest, it is also a necessary part of preparing the hero for the even greater challenges to come, often a path to gaining new knowledge, skill, clarity, conviction, or confidence. All of this is essential as the hero reaches a central challenge of the quest, facing the hero's greatest fear, walking on the edge of defeat. In fact, it might result in what seems like a complete failure, even death in many of the great myths of past and present. Having faced the greatest fear or challenge and overcome or survived it, the hero reaps a reward; then, the journey begins back to the ordinary world.

Some version of this narrative shows up in the greatest and most persistent myths of past and present. We see it in great Greek myths like *Hercules Labors* but also in some of the most beloved legends of the modern age: The *Star Wars* saga, *The Matrix*, and almost every well-known Disney movie.

While these elements might seem distant from what we think of as real-life or learning, they are not. These same elements of a grand quest are available to all of us, and they serve as a compelling framework for thinking about schools and other learning communities. We have calls to the special world in each of our lives. The question is whether we heed the call and whether we choose to look at the world around us through the lens of *The Hero's Journey*. As Joseph Campbell explains in many ways, the question is whether you will say yes to the calls to adventure in your life.

Remember that a quest only needs a clear and challenging goal, along with some milestones along the way. It might be a fitness or wellness journey, a fight for new knowledge, a crusade for having an impact on a specific problem in your life or community, a pursuit for a new career, or some new aspect of your current job. It can be almost anything. The same thing is true in schools.

I invite you to join me in reconsidering what a classroom or learning experience would look like created through this lens. Consider framing a student's journey in the following way. Once you have a clear mission and goal, consider using Joseph Campbell's description of *The Hero's Journey* to chart your course. Start by counting the cost. Are you ready to do what it takes for this quest, to venture into unchartered territory, beyond the safety of your current ordinary world? Are there guides or mentors to help you as you begin? What about allies? What are the enemies or barriers, and how will you overcome them? You get the idea. As human beings, we crave noble quests and adventures. By using the language and lens of the *Hero's Journey*, we will soon find ourselves infusing more oxygen into classrooms and schools.

> *"Security is mostly a superstition. It does not exist in nature, nor do the children of men as a whole experience it. Avoiding danger is no safer in the long run than outright exposure. Life is either a daring adventure or nothing."*
>
> — HELEN KELLER

Most importantly, remember that learners do not receive a call to anyone else's noble adventure, and it doesn't matter whether one learner finds another learner's pursuit noble, challenging, or inspiring. If the goal or mission is meaningful to that student, if it challenges that student, then it is a worthy quest. If we can identify how it intersects with a pressing need in a student's family, community, or world, even better.

> *"It's a dangerous business, Frodo, going out your door. You step onto the road, and if you don't keep your feet, there's no knowing where you might be swept off to."*
>
> — J.R.R. TOLKIEN

As an exercise in considering how to infuse this oxygen-rich element into a classroom, consider reflecting on the following questions:

- Are there calls to a quest in this course?

- How does this course support the existing or emerging quests of each learner?
- How can I use the language of quests and adventures in this course or learning community?
- What would my course look like as a quest or embedded into one or more quest-like narratives?
- Are there any elements of my course that minimize or muzzle a quest-based approach? How might I minimize or remove some of those barriers?

AGENCY AND ACTION

"Freedom is the oxygen of the soul."

— MOSHE DAYAN

What you say and do matters. It matters for you, the people around you, and the world. Your choices, words, and actions can create positive change in your life and the lives of the people around you. Knowing and believing this is what we call human agency. If you think that your words and actions don't matter much, then you will be less motivated to try to effect positive change. When you get to a place where you know that countless factors within your control can make the world better for you and others, that is powerful, meaningful, inspiring, and much needed in our communities. This is what we want for each learner in a modern school or learning community. Our world needs people who feel and think this way. Our democracy and collective well-being depend upon it happening.

This is why it is a crisis when our fixation of centralized power and control leaves no room for agency and action to grow and flourish. It can be frightening for an educator to step back or create space for a greater learner voice, choice, ownership, and agency, but the risks are well worth the rewards.

Agency grows when we feed it, and it thrives upon competence and confidence. In other words, you must grow in your belief that you can accomplish something, and you must grow in your actual ability to accomplish it. Whatever helps you grow in these two areas will aid you in recognizing how much power and influence you have in your learning and the rest of life. We must search for whatever can build learner competence and confidence as if it were a prized treasure. Better yet, we must strive to create learning communities where learners have the ownership and agency to search for whatever can build their competence and confidence. After all, that is what we see in the journey of anyone who achieves a world-class level of performance. These world-class performers often have coaches and others who guide and direct them at different stages, but the world-class performers are not just following instructions. They are taking the initiative and seeking out that which will get them where they want to be one day. That is the mindset that we want to cultivate in our schools.

The importance of agency does not ignore the reality that there are factors beyond our control. Whether they are what some might consider cosmic injustices (e.g., not having the genes to be seven feet tall), or systemic injustices (unjust laws or inequities in society), there is still a reality that the person with a deep sense of agency has a better chance of effecting the desired personal and social change.

How do you nurture agency in a school? Consider three simple starting points. First, recognize each learner's passions and desires. What do the learners want to accomplish in their lives and the world? Try not to censor learners when describing these. Next, invite each learner to make some plans on how to accomplish one of those things. Look at how others have done it. Maybe even talk to and interview them. Find examples of people with whom they can relate. Explore different strategies and approaches. As one's knowledge grows, one's confidence will as well. Third, guide the learners in setting some goals. Based upon what they learned from their planning stage, invite them to set goals that will let them know if they are making progress. Invite them to start with small goals that they can accomplish more easily. This will build their confidence and their competence for the more challenging goals.

Do this over and over. The more they do, the more they will grow in their belief that they can indeed change the situations in their lives. They will have a growing set of personal examples that their thoughts, plans, goals, and actions make a tangible difference.

"What oxygen is to the lungs, such is hope to the meaning of life."

— EMIL BRUNNER

Here are a few questions to consider when trying to infuse the oxygen of agency into a classroom:

- How can I engage each of the learners in

determining and prioritizing what they need and want to learn?

- How can I engage each of the learners in determining how they are going to monitor their progress along the way?
- How can I engage each of the learners in determining how best to accomplish the established priorities?
- How can I provide a supportive environment where learners are taking greater ownership of what they learn, how they learn it, and even why they need to learn it?

COMPASSION AND CONNECTEDNESS

"Basic human contact—the meeting of eyes, the exchanging of words—is to the psyche what oxygen is to the brain. If you're feeling abandoned by the world, interact with anyone you can."

— MARTHA BECK

Whether or not you are a religious person, there is a fascinating part of the creation account in the book of Genesis. After God creates Adam, and before sin enters the world, there is this moment when God says, "It is not good for man to be alone." The story goes on to describe that God addressed this matter by creating woman. People might read all sorts of things into this story and its intended lessons, but consider this simple yet profound truth in this story: people do not exist to be alone. We are relational beings. Some might be more extraverted or introverted, but everyone craves and needs meaningful connections with others.

From our entry into this world as babies, we need relationships with other humans to survive. The development of infants is improved by the touch of a loving caregiver. As we become older and more independent, this need for others might seem less necessary or obvious, but it remains. You can ask neuroscientists, biologists, psychologists, or sociologists, and the consensus will be the same. While people might be able to survive in isolation, and while times of solitude can be healing and useful, we need human interaction to be at our best.

Perhaps this is why some people endure less than healthy connections with others instead of facing the perceived fear of being alone. While not recommended, we can recognize why it is a temptation to tolerate abuse or mistreatment. What we thrive upon, however, is creating meaningful and positive connections with others.

While sincere and lasting friendships and relationships are a good and essential part of this need for connection, we can't discount the power of small moments of human contact as well. We might enjoy a brief exchange of smiles with a stranger, an enjoyable interaction with the barista, small talk while waiting in line at the store, a positive collaboration with colleague on a project at work, the spontaneous aid of a stranger in a time of need, or a short word of gratitude for someone in our life.

A growing body of research indicates that people who have and maintain strong social connections not only report greater feelings of well-being, they are healthier and live longer. Positive social interaction with others and having social support from one or more communities appear to reduce inflammation, improve blood pressure, decrease stress hormones, and mitigate against common health concerns.

Given such a deep, fundamental, and beneficial craving

for positive human connections, there are few areas of our life worthy of a greater investment of our time and energy. Deepening meaningful connections offers a treasure trove of benefits that far exceed the promise of wealth, career, and so many other aspects of modern life that occupy our time. This is not to diminish the value or benefits of these other areas, and as I am finding myself restating throughout this book, there need not be an either-or approach.

If you are seeking a life rich with meaning, purpose, and well-being, then placing friends, family, and positive relationships at the top of your priority list is a wise move. Interview a thousand people near the end of their life, and you are unlikely to find a single person lamenting having spent too much time with a family member, friends, or other people. A 2012 *Forbes* magazine article pulled together the twenty-five greatest regrets in life, and the first on the list was, "Working so much at the expense of family and friends." Of the other twenty-five, eighteen were about relationships, particularly family and friends. This is one of those truths that we all come to see and believe at some point in our lives. The quest is whether we recognize it and prioritize it enough in the present so that we find our lives enriched now, and we enjoy the fruit of that effort to the end of our lives.

"*Compassion is the keen awareness of the interdependence of all things.*"

— THOMAS MERTON

Consider the following questions as a way of infusing the oxygen of connection and compassion into learning communities:

- How many authentic and meaningful connections do learners make with the educator, other learners, or other potential mentors?
- How can we redesign or reimagine the learning community so that there are frequent and meaningful connections between learners?
- Since grading and feedback are often a significant form of communication between teacher and learner, can how we humanize this interaction, turning it into an opportunity for mentoring and coaching more than rating and ranking?
- How can we reimagine feedback as an opportunity for peers to connect in meaningful, positive, and mutually beneficial ways?
- What will it take to create a learning community where learners are proactively reaching out to, encouraging, supporting, and collaborating with one another in meaningful and authentic ways?

EXPERIMENTATION AND PLAY

"A child who does not play is not a child, but the man who does not play has lost forever the child who lived in him."

— PABLO NERUDA

I magine an activity that can increase productivity at work and school, speed the rate and depth of learning something new, increase well-being and satisfaction, decrease stress, enhance the bonding between two or more people, and strengthen connections and communication with others. With such a long list of benefits, who wouldn't want to engage? The activity that I'm describing is play.

Stuart Brown, a leading expert on the merits of play, argues that "Play is a basic human need as essential to our well-being as sleep, so when we're low on play, our minds and bodies notice..." If this is true, then play is certainly not just for children, nor is it best reserved for a special treat. If humans fundamentally crave play, then it is best made a part of our daily lives and the daily lives of learners.

Yet, there is an ongoing tension about the word "play" for many people. In both schools and work, there continue to be some who are skeptical about anything that uses the word play. School and work are about productivity and hard work, and people think of play as something different. Turning again to Stuart Brown, he reminds us that, "the opposite of play is not work, it is depression."

When we diminish the value of playfulness in schools and workplaces, where many of us spend a significant part of our lives, we are depriving ourselves and others of something deeply inspiring and invigorating, something that we crave and helps us to achieve well-being and higher levels of productivity.

While distinct, experimentation often flows out of play and playfulness. In imaginative play, we venture beyond the present world as we see and experience it. We find ourselves experimenting with other possibilities, even if only in our minds. Experiments are, in one sense, tests that we conduct to explore some thesis, question, or examine a possibility. They often grow out of a willingness to ask and wonder. Some of the most compelling questions in human history led to both play and experimentation but went on to discovery and transformation.

Ray Bradbury once wrote, "life is trying things to see if they work." Ralph Waldo Emerson similarly wrote, "All life is an experiment. The more experiments you make, the better." While the scientists among us have more narrow definitions for what constitutes a good one, it is the orientation toward experimentation that matters. To experiment is to test something out, whenever possible, in the real world. You have an idea of how things might be, and you conduct one or more experiments. You observe and seek actionable insights that often lead to more experiments.

To experiment is to learn, and it taps into that drive for adventure that we already explored. Every true experiment is an adventure because you don't know the outcome. Experiments have that sense of wild, curiosity, uncertainty, and mystery, and these are things upon which people thrive.

You don't need formal training to start, although many tools can help. In fact, you've been experimenting your entire life. You conducted an experiment the first time you tried to walk and each time after that. You experimented when you tried to reach out and touch that intriguing red stovetop. You experimented when you stuck your tongue out to catch your first snowflake and to figure out how to get your bicycle to stay upright while you pedal. You conducted an experiment when you tasted something new, tried to improve on a video game, or explored people's reactions to your words and actions. Maybe you didn't start every endeavor with a hypothesis, but each of these is an expression of experimentation.

People continue to experiment throughout their lives, but over time, we find comfort in something quite different. We develop rituals and habits. We find ourselves drawn to safe and stable situations where we are already confident about the outcomes. Think of how often we design classrooms in this same way. Experiments entail risks, and the yearning for safety and security competes with the equally important yearning for novelty, adventure, and learning.

There is nothing wrong with safety, and rituals are rich, beautiful, and meaningful parts of our lives. Or, even when they are not, they serve other useful purposes in our lives. The problem is when the pull for safety and security begins to close us off from the experimenting part of learning.

It helps to make experimentation a more planned and intentional part of the learning community. One way to do this is through what I call life experiments. These are simple processes intended to test out new practices, ideas, and activities. For example, if you find yourself struggling with negativity, what if you conducted a simple experiment for ten days in a row where you end each day by writing three things that went well and why. This particular practice comes from Martin Seligman, the father of positive psychology, finding that something as simple as this can greatly improve the optimism and sense of well-being for many people. Of course, you don't know if it will work for you unless you try it, perhaps you can test it out for ten days and see for yourself. You can do the same thing with experiments around building new relationships, setting and achieving goals, managing your time, or getter better at a hobby or a skill for work. Now imagine a classroom or learning community of students who are persistently creating simple experiments for themselves and others, gaining new experiences and insights, and using that to learn and grow in new ways.

Some students will be hesitant, not having engaged in this sort of playfulness or experimentation. Here are three simple suggestions to get started. First, have the learners begin by exploring something they want to understand or improve or a problem they want to solve. Maybe they want to understand better how to make money, get along with a sibling, improve a skill in a sport, address a troubling social issue, or how to develop a new ability.

Next, create a context where they can read, talk to people, watch documentaries and YouTube videos, and gain some new knowledge about the area of interest. As they learn and explore, they will start to find possibilities and practices that intrigue the learners. That is where we go to step two. Have each learner create a simple, time-based experiment that allows them to learn, through direct experience, how that practice or possibility might work in their life or the world. For example, several years ago, Martin Seligman and others popularized findings of a study that revealed the power of a simple bedtime practice. Before going to sleep, write down three things that went well that day and why. I read this and decided to give it a try. I committed to doing it daily for four weeks. At the end of each day, I also wrote down how I felt: bad, okay, good, or amazing. At the end of the four weeks, I went back, reviewed my statements about the day, and I tallied up how many days I felt bad, okay, good, and amazing. I probably should have recorded how I felt daily for a month before starting. I didn't. Regardless, the pattern was clear. In week one of my little life experiment, I felt bad two days, okay on four days, and good on one day. At the end of week four, I felt bad one day, okay one day, good three days, and amazing on two days. Given the positive outcome, I decided to continue with the practice or different versions of it, which leads to the third suggestion.

Once learners identify something to explore and conduct an experiment, they can make it their goal to gain actionable insight about themselves, the topic, the problem, or the world. It isn't simply about whether it worked or not. There are lessons to be learned regardless of the outcome. This is where some form of personal reflection is valuable. This can be as simple as posing a few questions to oneself and pondering them. I tend to create times throughout for reflection, dedicating a more extended time in the end. In addition, I always include some sort of question like, "What next?" In other words, now that the experiment is complete, what do I want to do with the insights? I might continue the experiment, make some adjustments to my life in some way, or get an idea for a new or related experiment.

This should be fun, even playful. They are exploring and experimenting. Some might enjoy inviting others to join them in creating and conducting personal life experiments, sharing their lessons and insights along the way. Others might prefer keeping them private. I'm offering a few suggestions, but engage the learners to decide what to do, when to do it, and how to do it.

In some ways, this recipe approach might feel "industrial" in nature. As I've mentioned before, those are not bad values. We just need to gain control of the values and make sure we prioritize and celebrate the deeply human-centered ones. That is what we are doing here. We are creating a recipe that helps you prioritize more experimentation and play in your life.

By adding more play and experimentation into our learning communities, we are embracing a sense of possibility, and possibility breeds hope and a deeper sense of meaning. As Paul Rogat Loeb wrote, "Possibility is the oxygen upon which hope thrives."

H ere are a few questions for further consideration:

- How much do learners presently play and experiment in the classroom or learning community?
- What are simple ways for learners to engage in the content or learning goals through structured or unstructured play?
- How can I infuse more playfulness into the

classroom or learning community? What ideas might students have for this?

- How can I invite learners to take a posture of experimentation about their learning but also about seeking an understanding of other things that are important in their lives?

MASTERY AND GROWTH

"Mastery is not a function of genius or talent. It is a function of time and intense focus applied to a particular field of knowledge."

— ROBERT GREENE

An industrial model of learning is more about repetition and fitting into the mold. It is about growing in the pot in which someone planted you. People thrive when they are free to grow beyond the size of their current pot. Growth is an expression of vibrant life.

The opposite is stagnation. While some think that survival is the goal, inspiration goes from surviving to thriving. Thriving is always about developing, new experiences, pursuing new goals, achieving new skills, and knowledge useful in achieving personally meaningful goals. As Abraham Maslow wrote, "You will either step forward into growth, or you will step back into safety."

So much of our thinking about growth and mastery is tainted by how the education system conditioned us to think about learning. In fact, it isn't even about learning much of the time. As we already discussed, it is about earning a grade or reaching a certain number of points. For many people, school is about earning more than it is about learning, which loses sight of the very purpose of learning. Learning, growth, and mastery are each about something else. We seek to develop new skills when we have a purpose that compels us to do so. We achieve mastery when we are on an adventure or quest that calls for us to become something else. We experience a moment of wonder, which leads to curiosity, and that drives us to grow or learn something new.

Growth and mastery lose their meaning when separated from all these other deeply human yearnings. When they are present, however, we find that growth and mastery flow from them. If I don't have a reason to read, why would I put the time and effort into mastering the necessary skills? Someone might require or force me to go through the motions, and perhaps I respect—or fear—that person enough to do it. Eventually, one of two things happen in such a situation. One, the person who forced us to do it is no longer around, so we quit and forget. Or, somewhere along the way, we discover a purpose, mission, or quest that helps us discover a personally meaningful reason to learn it. Then it is no longer about what someone else wants us to do. We have an internal motivation that drives us.

While many of us think that schools focus on growth and mastery, these questions will help surface some ways to do it in a more authentic and oxygen-infusing manner:

- How can I create a space or system where students get authentic feedback on their work from people beyond the classroom or school?
- How can I invite learners to compare their work to people who are experts or world-class in that respect?
- How can I invite learners to think and talk about their learning in terms of personal growth and mastery and less in terms of points and grades?
- How can I create learning experiences where learners are comparing their present work to what they accomplished in the past? In what ways is the new work better or worse than before?

MEANING AND PURPOSE

Years ago, while pursuing my doctoral degree, a professor of qualitative research told us the story of a study conducted on why college students fall asleep in class. The researcher used a methodology called grounded theory. You start with a question, identify a sample of people relevant to your question—in this case, people who fell asleep in college classes—and then you interview them one at a time. As you collect insights from each new person that you speak with, you develop a tentative theory about your question. Then you interview more people, testing to see if your theory holds up under the new insights. Based upon what you learn along the way, you continue to adjust your theory until it explains the phenomenon common to the sample of people you interviewed. This might take fifteen to twenty-five in-depth conversations.

In this case, the researcher concluded the study with an answer to the question about falling asleep in class. It came down to two words. It didn't have to do with the effectiveness of the instructor—at least not directly—the health or sleeping habits of the learners, or the difficulty of the class. The theory that held up across all the board was that college students are most likely to fall asleep in class when they experience "perceived meaninglessness."

Notice that it did not have to do with the course content, whether the instructor was entertaining, the time of day, or any such matters. It came down to a deeply personal and subjective matter. Did the learner perceive what was happening in that class as meaningful? With meaning, comes interest and motivation. Without it, we struggle, lose interest, disconnect, and find ourselves experiencing those symptoms of oxygen deficiency again.

"The mystery of human existence lies not in just staying alive, but in finding something to live for."

— Fyodor Dostoyevsky

It isn't the circumstance as much as it is whether learners see meaning or purpose in it. As a teacher for well over twenty years, I'm embarrassed to admit that it took me almost fifteen years to understand the implications of this truth. Why is it, for example, that some learners thrive in courses where the teacher embodies the passion of a rock or displays a lack of observable teaching skills? Usually, if you find many people thriving in such a course, or at least persisting and learning a great deal, it is because they are approaching and enduring that course with meaning and purpose. Maybe they are medical students who have a clear goal of becoming physicians, and they know that this course, however poorly taught, is between them and their goal. They have a vision for what they want to accomplish or whom they want to be, and they see this course, or the learning provided in the course as a step toward making that vision a reality. The vision gives meaning and purpose to the course. "Where there is no vision, the people perish" (Proverbs 29:19).

Great educators find ways to help people discover meaning and purpose in a course. Still, the real magic comes when learners discover how to create or identify meaning and purpose for themselves. That is a life skill that will bless and befriend that student far beyond formal schooling.

This is nothing new to most educators. Anyone who studied education in college learned about the importance of having a hook or anticipatory set at the beginning of a lesson. The goal of a hook is to capture the attention of the learners. Only, the flaw with this approach is that it is often teacher-centered in its design, or it is an educated guess. What will "hook" some learners will not interest others. As such, a learning community infused with the oxygen of meaning and purpose creates an environment where every learner is connecting with something meaningful.

"So what?" That is a question that any educator has heard or asked. It is a question asked by every learner. It is a question about why a body of content, lesson, or idea matters. Where is the meaning? What is the purpose? Even if one is working in a traditional classroom setting, the minimum advice is to at least linger on the so what. In other words, don't just give a quick hook and move on to the lesson. That is just going through the motions. If we want an inspired classroom, then it calls for taking as much time as needed to help people understand, embrace, or create some sort of personally meaningful reason to engage in the learning ahead. Better to take four days on the so what and one day on the main lesson if that is what it takes for people to be deeply interested, engaged in, and committed to the learning of that one day.

Of course, the more often schools invite the learners into creating or co-creating what happens, the easier it becomes to find meaning and purpose. In addition, inviting learners into judging or discovering the meaning and purpose of a topic can seem time-consuming, but it produces immense rewards when we see the difference it makes in learner interest and engagement.

Here are some questions to consider in the pursuit of such a learning community:

- How can I help learners discover a personally compelling reason for learning this?
- How can I invite learners to create or discover the meaning and purpose in the lesson?
- What would it look like to linger on the so what until all students are connected?
- What different approaches to teaching and learning might be most useful in accomplishing this?
- How can I create learning experiences that connect directly with what is already meaningful to each learner?

WONDER AND MYSTERY

"Look up at the stars and not down at your feet. Try to make sense of what you see and wonder about what makes the universe exist. Be curious."

— STEPHEN HAWKING

Holding a newborn child. Witnessing a sunrise. Listening to a masterful musical performance. Watching an athlete at the brink of what we thought humanly possible and then seeing her breakthrough to an entirely new level. Discovering the pattern in a seemingly random set of numbers. After years of searching, gazing upon a rare and beautiful endangered species. Sitting outside and seeing something familiar as if you were looking at it for the first time, only this time, a beautiful, distinct, and awe-inspiring feature captures your attention. Witnessing an incredible act of kindness or sacrifice. These are just a few of the possibilities for how wonder finds its way into our lives.

We experience many things in our lives, most that we forget, but when we experience moments of wonder, they stay with us so much so that they become a permanent part of us. They are often the type of memories that not only last for years and decades, but those recollections retain a vividness that exceeds impressions of what happened to us two days ago. A human experience that powerful demands our respect and attention. Why wouldn't we want more wonder in our schools? Why would we ignore such an incredible potential force for good in our lives and learning?

While many think of wonder as a rare and fleeting moment, it is entirely possible to cultivate an outlook on life where it is a daily occurrence. It isn't as much about what you see, hear, or sense; it is about *how* you see, hear, and sense. What is experienced by one person as the mundane and ordinary is treasured by another as awe-inspiring. While it is difficult to explain how it happens, the pursuit of such an outlook is worth the sacrifice. Imagine going through life with weekly, if not daily, moments that linger, inspire, and spur your imagination.

A growing body of research on the psychology of wonder gives us an even greater appreciation of its role in our world. When people experience a moment of wonder, they are more open to respecting those who are different. The humility that comes from such moments influences how we treat others. The benefits continue. Moments of wonder evoke generosity, a decreased sense of entitlement, not to mention some reports that these experiences can help us heal from past trauma. To experience wonder is to feel alive, inspired, and part of something bigger than oneself.

Some distinguish between wonder as a noun and a verb. As a noun, it is that moment of surprise combined with admiration. It leaves you still, entranced, and living in that moment. You are feeling and experiencing without much conscious analysis. You feel humility, even a sense of smallness. From such moments often comes the experience of wonder as a verb. This is where your stillness and awe inspire your mind to ponder, to inquire, to explore. You begin to ask questions about how and why, and if you have the agency to learn, you find yourself motivated to understand and to explore. You experience a curiosity conjured by a vivid and persistent moment.

"I am a great admirer of mystery and magic. Look at this life—all mystery and magic."

— HARRY HOUDINI

We naturally want to learn, explore, to solve problems; and mysteries stir our yearning for both adventure and meaning. Show someone a partially completed picture and their brain is likely to fill in the gaps. A growing body of research validates this drive to some puzzles, and it points us to the larger reality about the human experience. We expect there to be meaning and an explanation in the world around us, so when someone presents us with the unexplained, the unsolved problem, we are often drawn into its mystery.

The first library book that I remember picking up was in the first grade at a small school library. It was an over-sized book, full of pictures and stories about haunted houses. Then there was the book nearby about UFOs with another one about the legends of the Loch Ness Monster. I could look at those books for hours. I was less interested in reading them, but they drew me into this world of questions and enigmas.

These books pointed me to the fact that we live in a world of unexplained puzzles and possibilities, sometimes too easy to forget. While there is much that we know, there is so much more that we do not. We walk through a world of unexplored, unexplained, partly explained, misunderstood, and misrepresented mysteries. Just when we think that we have learned something new, we begin to discover how much more we do not know.

Modern education can sometimes push us into a world of memorizing and understanding the hunted, shot, and stuffed facts of the past. The risk is turning learning and life into a museum tour instead of a wonderfully unpredictable lifelong adventure. We must learn what is known, but also be reminded of how much we don't know. Unanswered questions, conundrums, problems, and ambiguities provoke the much-needed virtue of curiosity. If nurtured, it can bloom into a lifelong love of learning that drives us to solve some of the greatest mysteries in our lives and the world, to discover new answers to questions, to bring clarity amid ambiguity.

Ask scholars or deeply informed students about what most interests them about their work. You will almost always find such people talking about questions, unsolved puzzles, the unknown or partly unknown, the ambiguities and paradoxes of their study. Ask any entrepreneur a similar question. Often it will reside with challenges they face, goals they have yet to achieve, and questions they grapple to answer. That is because learning is fueled by questions more than answers. As Neil Armstrong said, "Mystery creates wonder and wonder is the basis of man's desire to understand."

Mystery and wonder are beautifully connected. They feed one another, creating the oxygen that fuels our roles as lifelong learners, explorers, inventors, and creators. They help us connect with some of our greatest and most persistent yearnings.

H ere are a few questions to help begin to consider ways to infuse the power of wonder and mysteries into your classroom:

- Where are the unsolved mysteries in this subject?
- What are the ideas and experiences in this field that have intrigued and inspired many scholars to devote their lives to the area of study? How can I help learners begin to see the field from the perspective of such scholars?
- How can I turn declarative statements and facts into intriguing puzzles?
- What are the challenges or feats yet to be accomplished in the world? Or, metaphorically speaking, what are the unclimbed mountains?
- What are the accomplished feats that leave you awe-struck and inspired?
- How can we create or pursue the wonder-full together?

CONCLUSION

We live in a world of industrial priorities, and at least as we think about modern life, it is hard to deny their value in the world. Standards, numbers, and efficiencies have their place. These and the other industrial priorities are not the enemies. It is just that they don't offer a solid foundation. They are most valuable when used in the service of something greater, something much more deeply human.

That is where the seven fundamental human appetites in this book come into play. They are far from an exhaustive list. I could have also devoted time to a celebration and call to what some refer to as the transcendentals of truth, beauty, and goodness. These, too, are deeply human and oxygen-generating values. We could have looked at many other ideas from research and different wisdom traditions. As such, I offer the seven in this book as a starting point for our investment in humanizing priorities and values, not as an exhaustive list. In fact, in the spirit of adventure, let it be a personal quest to discover and explore other deeply human priorities, ones that infuse our schools and our communities with the kind of intellectual and emotional air that we crave and breathe.

Ancient wisdom and modern research point us to what we crave. We yearn for qualities like adventure and quests, agency and action, compassion and meaningful connections, experimentation and play, mastery and growth, meaning and purpose, as well as wonder and mystery. The more that we breathe these into our learning communities, the more we begin to experience inspired learning.

Now is the time to breathe...

To experiment...

To play...

To explore...

To learn...

To live.

ABOUT THE AUTHOR

Dr. Bernard Bull is Founder & CEO of Birdhouse Learning Labs and President of Goddard College. He previously served as Chief Innovation Officer, Vice Provost of Curriculum and Innovation, and Professor of Education at Concordia University Wisconsin. His applied research focuses upon futures in education, learner agency and ownership, self-directed learning, human-centered learning experience design, and the intersection of education and digital culture.

You can follow his work at www.etale.org.

 twitter.com/BernardBull

Made in the USA
Monee, IL
04 November 2021

81440844R00059